Gateway Arch

ABDO
Publishing Company

A Buddy Book
by
Julie Murray

VISIT US AT
www.abdopub.com

Published by Buddy Books, an imprint of ABDO Publishing Company, 4940 Viking Drive, Edina, Minnesota 55435. Copyright © 2003 by Abdo Consulting Group, Inc. International copyrights reserved in all countries. No part of this book may be reproduced in any form without written permission from the publisher.

Printed in the United States.

Edited by: Christy DeVillier
Contributing Editors: Matt Ray, Michael P. Goecke
Graphic Design: Deborah Coldiron
Image Research: Deborah Coldiron
Cover Photograph: PhotoSpin
Interior Photographs: Corbis, Getty Images, Photodisc

Library of Congress Cataloging-in-Publication Data

Murray, Julie, 1969-
    Gateway Arch / Julie Murray.
        p. cm. — (All aboard America)
    Includes index.
    Summary: Discusses the construction, history, and current status of the Gateway Arch in Saint Louis, Missouri, which is a memorial to the city's role in pioneer days.
    ISBN 1-57765-671-7
        1. Gateway Arch (Saint Louis, Mo.)—Juvenile literature. 2. Arches—Missouri—Saint Louis—Design and construction—Juvenile literature. [1. Gateway Arch (Saint Louis, Mo.)—History. 2. Saint Louis (Mo.)—Buildings, structures, etc.] I. Title.

TA660.A7 M87 2002
725'.96—dc21

                                                        2001055218

Table of Contents

CHAPTER 1

Gateway Arch

The Gateway Arch is the tallest **monument** in the United States. It is 630 feet (192 m) tall. The arch is twice as tall as the Statue of Liberty. The Gateway Arch stands near the Mississippi River in St. Louis, Missouri.

The Gateway Arch (GAYT-way arch) stands by the Mississippi River.

The Gateway Arch is part of the Jefferson National Expansion **Memorial**. This memorial honors the American West of the 1800s.

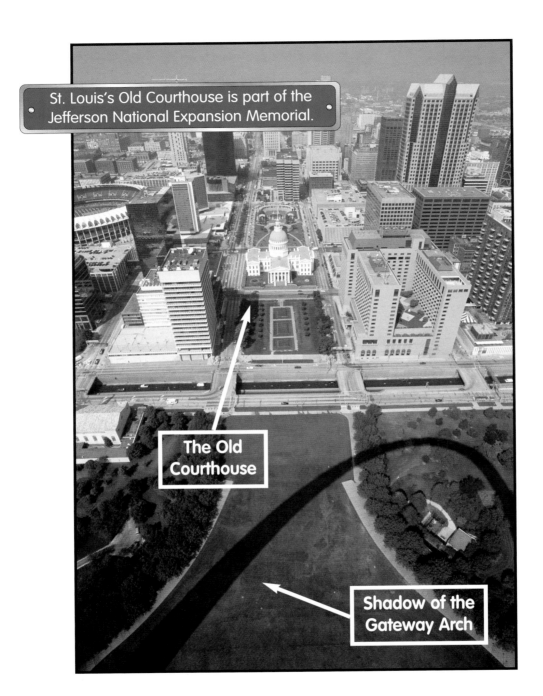

St. Louis's Old Courthouse is part of the Jefferson National Expansion Memorial.

The Old Courthouse

Shadow of the Gateway Arch

The Jefferson National Expansion Memorial was named after President Thomas Jefferson.

Long ago, St. Louis was on the edge of America's western **frontier**. People began calling St. Louis the Gateway to the West. This is why the Jefferson National Expansion **Memorial** is in St. Louis. And this is how the Gateway Arch got its name.

Detour

Did You Know?

The Gateway Arch is as tall as a 63-story building.

The Jefferson National Expansion **Memorial** Association was in charge of the memorial. They thought it should have a museum, a park, and a **monument**. In 1947, they held a contest to find the best monument idea. Eero Saarinen sent in his idea of a great steel arch. Saarinen won the contest.

Eero Saarinen

Eero Saarinen was born in Finland in 1910. He moved to the United States in 1923. Saarinen studied to be an **architect** like his father. He went to the Yale School of Architecture. The Gateway Arch was Saarinen's first big success.

Saarinen also worked on Washington Dulles International Airport near Washington, D.C.

The building of the Gateway Arch began on February 12, 1963. Workers dug a deep hole for the arch's **foundation**. The foundation is 60 feet (18 m) deep in the ground. This helps the arch stand up against strong winds.

Did You Know?

It cost $13 million to build the Gateway Arch.

The Gateway Arch has 142 steel sections. It is made of 900 tons (816 t) of stainless steel. This giant arch weighs 17,246 tons (15,645 t).

The Gateway Arch was built to withstand 150-mph (241-kph) winds.

The Gateway Arch is made of steel.

It took two and a half years to build the Gateway Arch. It was finished on October 28, 1965.

Mississippi river boats pass by the Gateway Arch all the time.

Over one million people ride to the top of the Gateway Arch each year.

The Gateway Arch is the star of the Jefferson National Expansion **Memorial**. The view from the top of the arch is amazing. People can see St. Louis and western Illinois. On a clear day, people can see for 30 miles (48 km).

How do people get to the top of the Gateway Arch? A tram takes them there. There are two trams inside the arch. Forty people can ride in each tram. Riding to the top takes about four minutes. Thousands of people ride to the top of the Gateway Arch each day.

Detour ⬇

Did You Know?

Lightning strikes the Gateway Arch hundreds of times each year.

The great Gateway Arch stands tall over St. Louis.

The Jefferson National Expansion **Memorial** has an underground visitor's center. The center shows movies about how the Gateway Arch was built. The Museum of Westward Expansion is there, too.

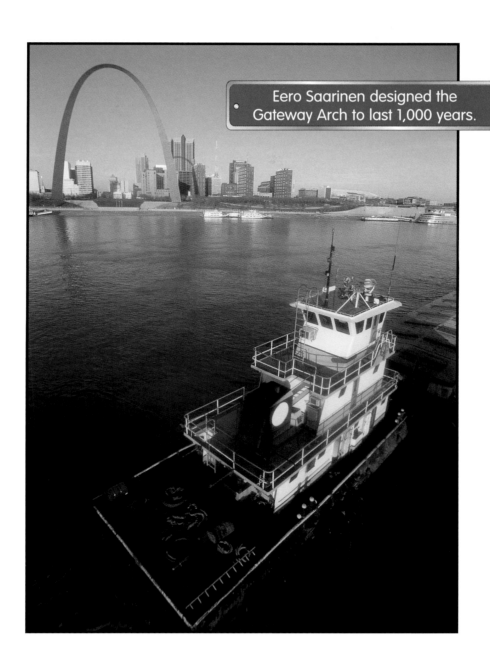

Eero Saarinen designed the Gateway Arch to last 1,000 years.

Important Words

architect (AR-kuh-tekt) a person who designs buildings, bridges, and other things.

foundation (fown-DAY-shun) the base that helps to support a building or structure.

frontier (FRUN-teer) land that has not been settled by people.

memorial (muh-MOR-ree-ul) something that reminds people of a special person or event. A memorial can be a monument, a park, or a holiday.

monument (MON-yoo-munt) something built to remind people of a special person or event.

Web Sites

Would you like to learn more about the Gateway Arch?

Please visit ABDO Publishing Company on the information superhighway to find web site links about the Gateway Arch. These links are routinely monitored and updated to provide the most current information available.

www.abdopub.com

Index